Robert Quackenbush

CLARA BARTON

AND HER VICTORY OVER FEAR

SIMON & SCHUSTER BOOKS FOR YOUNG READERS

SIMON & SCHUSTER BOOKS FOR YOUNG READERS
An imprint of Simon & Schuster Children's Publishing Division
1230 Avenue of the Americas, New York, New York 10020
Copyright © 1995 by Robert Quackenbush
All rights reserved including the right of reproduction
in whole or in part in any form.
SIMON & SCHUSTER BOOKS FOR YOUNG READERS
is a trademark of Simon & Schuster.
Book design by Robert Quackenbush.
The text for this book is set in 14-point Times Roman.
The illustrations were done in charcoal line and painted
in gouache mixed with acrylic gel.
Manufactured in the United States of America

10 9 8 7 6 5 4 3 2 1

Library of Congress Cataloging-in-Publication Data
Quackenbush, Robert M. Clara Barton and her victory over fear / Robert Quackenbush.
p. cm. Includes bibliographical references. 1. Barton, Clara, 1821–1912—Juvenile literature.
2. Red Cross—United States—Biography—Juvenile literature. 3. Nurses—United States—
Biography—Juvenile literature. [1. Barton, Clara, 1821–1912. 2. Nurses.
3. American National Red Cross.] I. Title. HV569.B3Q33 1995
361.7′634′092—dc20 [B] 94-18168 CIP AC
ISBN: 0-671-86598-6

FOR MARGIE
who is dedicated to helping people find their way

AND FOR PIET
who has learned the value of keeping a journal

CLARA, AT AGE THREE, RACES ON HORSEBACK WITHOUT A SADDLE

Clarissa Harlowe Barton was born on December 25, 1821, in a small, white cottage on a hill in North Oxford, Massachusetts. From the time she could talk, she called herself Clara. Her parents, Sara Stone Barton and Captain Stephen Barton, were prosperous farmers. Clara was the youngest of five children. Her sisters Sally and Dorothy were ten and seventeen, and her brothers David and Stephen were thirteen and fifteen when she was born.

For Clara, having brothers and sisters so much older was like having additional parents. Throughout her childhood, her life was disciplined by six grownups. Clara's mother taught her to sew, cook, and make soap, and how to run a busy household. Her father, who fought in the French and Indian War, taught her American history and how to memorize military ranks and the various government offices. Sally and Dorothy, both teachers, taught her to read. Stephen, a noted mathematician, taught her arithmetic. David—Clara's favorite—was a natural athlete and taught her to ride horseback when she was only three years old.

In spite of all Clara learned to do, she was painfully timid and shy. There were many reasons for this. As the only child in a family of grownups, she felt that her own needs were not important. She was unable to speak out and ask for things. She had no playmates with whom she could identify or compete. "In the earliest years of my life, I remember nothing but fear," said Clara in her memoirs.

CLARA, AT AGE FOUR, IS FRIGHTENED BY AN APPROACHING STORM

Many things frightened Clara as a child. When she was barely two-and-a-half years old, she was terrified by a snake that she saw slithering near the stoop where she was playing. Another time, she wandered into the barn where some farm hands were about to butcher an ox. One of the men hit the ox on the head with an ax. The sight so horrified Clara that she fainted. Later, she said that she felt as if she herself had been struck. From an early age, Clara showed empathy for the suffering of others, which became part of her character.

Clara recalled in vivid detail another frightening experience when she was a small child. A relative of her family had died. The funeral services were held four miles away. All the household attended except for Clara and her brother David, who was assigned to look after her. David left the house for a moment, just as a sudden thunder shower was approaching. Looking up from a window, Clara saw massive rifts of clouds rolling in the sky and lightning darting among them like blazing fires. The clouds reminded her of a huge, old ram on the farm, of which she was very frightened. It was as though Clara had placed all her childhood fears onto the ram. "My terrors transformed those rising, rolling clouds into a whole heaven full of angry rams, marching down on me," said Clara. She began screaming. David tore back into the house and rushed to her side to reassure her. But the memory of how frightened she had been remained with her forever.

When Clara started school, at age four, she was the youngest in the class. Her teacher, Colonel Richard Stone, was surprised to find out that she could spell hard words like *artichoke*. He placed her in the advanced spelling class. Although she kept up with the work, Clara remained withdrawn. Then, when Clara was eight, Colonel Stone took a post at another school farther away. Clara's parents sent her to board at his school, hoping that the separation from home would cure her of her timidity. Instead, Clara became so homesick that she could not eat. Her parents had to bring her back home.

Soon afterward, Captain Barton's favorite nephew, Jeremiah Learned, died, leaving a wife, four children, and a farm. Captain and Mrs. Barton purchased the farm to help the widow and sold their hill land to their sons. They took Clara with them and moved in with the Learneds. Clara's sisters stayed to keep house for their brothers.

Clara was excited about the move. When a painter came to restore the house, she lost her shyness and asked if she could help him. The painter taught her to mix colors, to wallpaper, and to paint. Clara was proud of the new skills she had learned. More than that, she was happy being away from the watchful eyes of six grownups. She became close friends with the Learned children. Together they explored the three hundred acres of farmland and had many adventures. "My life seemed very full for a little girl of eight years," she recalled years later.

CLARA BEGINS TO LOSE HER SHYNESS

CLARA LEARNS ABOUT NURSING BY CARING FOR HER BROTHER

When Clara was eleven, her brother David had an accident. While he was helping a neighbor to raise a barn, a weak floorboard he was standing on gave way. He fell feet first to the basement, a floor below. Even though no bones were broken, his body apparently suffered a grave shock, for he came down with a high fever. He was brought to his parents' home, where the fever ran on, and his condition grew worse. He wanted only his devoted Clara at his bedside. "He had been my ideal from earliest memory," said Clara. "I was distressed beyond measure at his condition. I had been his little protégée, his companion, and in his nervous wretchedness he clung to me."

For the next two years, Clara's school and play stopped so she could nurse David. But his health did not improve. Finally he agreed to try a clinic that promoted steam baths and other types of "water cures." In three weeks David's health was restored, and he returned home. No one can say with certainty what cured him, but one thing was clear to him: His little sister had willed him to live.

After David's recovery, Clara was free again. She had been initiated into the care of the sick in the two years she had nursed David. But the long period of isolation affected her development. During those two years, she had been to school only one-half day. Returning to school after such a long absence was a painful experience for her. "I had grown even more timid, shrinking, and sensitive in the presence of others," she later said.

When Clara was fifteen, she overheard her mother talking with a house guest. He was L. N. Fowler, a popular lecturer of the day on human behavior. He attempted to guide individuals toward pursuits that fit their temperaments. Clara's mother asked Fowler what she could do about Clara, who was still so shy. She told him how Clara had appeared without gloves one Sunday just as the family was leaving for church. When her mother had asked what became of her gloves, Clara said they wore out. Puzzled, her mother had said, "Why didn't you ask for new gloves?" At that, Clara burst into tears.

After hearing the story, Fowler said this about Clara: "The sensitive nature will always remain. She will never assert herself for herself—she will suffer wrong first—but for others she will be perfectly fearless." He suggested that Clara be given a class to teach when she was older.

Clara did not take offense at Fowler's remarks. Instead, she felt that he understood her. It was natural for her to think of teaching because Sally, Dorothy, and Stephen were teachers. At seventeen, she passed the necessary examinations. Afterward, she was swiftly appointed to a teaching position in North Oxford. She marched into the classroom the first day unafraid. She maintained her confidence by keeping a diary as an outlet for her thoughts, feelings, and deepest concerns. She was a well-liked and respected teacher for more than a dozen years. Then, desiring further education, she enrolled at Clinton Liberal Institute for teachers in upstate New York.

AT AGE SEVENTEEN, CLARA BECOMES A TEACHER

CLARA WITH HER FIRST STUDENTS AT THE PUBLIC SCHOOL SHE ESTABLISHED

At Clinton Institute, Clara attracted suitors because of her poise and sense of humor gained from her years of teaching. She turned down all marriage proposals, however. "I could be more useful to the world by being free from matrimonial ties," she said. One disappointed suitor left for California. He struck it rich during the Gold Rush of 1849 and deposited $10,000 in a bank account in Clara's name. Clara refused to touch the money until years later when she used it for humanitarian work.

After graduating from Clinton, Clara went to visit a friend, Mary Norton, in Hightown, New Jersey. She found lodgings in nearby Bordentown and began teaching at a "subscription school." Wealthy people supported these schools, and parents of the students paid the teachers' salaries. Since poor people could not afford to pay the teachers, their children were barred from these schools, and there were no public schools in the area to accommodate them. This situation infuriated Clara and she decided to do something about it. She went before the school board, offering to open the town's first public school. She would receive no wages until the school board was satisfied that it was a success.

Thus, in 1852, she became mistress of a shabby schoolhouse. Six boys she found sitting on a fence became her first students. The next day more children from poor families came to Clara's school. Then students from subscription schools came because they heard Clara was such a good teacher. Clara began to receive a salary. Enrollment grew so large that she had to bring in additional teachers to help her.

Within two years the enrollment at Clara's school reached six hundred, and she required a larger building. A brand new public school was built. The school board brought in a young, male principal to run the school and paid him more than twice what they were paying Clara. Clara was in turn demoted to "female assistant." She knew that the decision was based on her gender and not on her skill. To make matters worse, the new principal proceeded to establish strict rules for the children, of which Clara did not approve. The environment became so unbearable that Clara decided to resign from the school in 1854. Ill and exhausted, she left Bordentown to stay with her sister Sally, who was now married and living in Washington, D.C.

Clara recovered her health in Washington. Through the efforts of a distant relative, a Massachusetts congressman, she found employment and moved into her own apartment. She was hired as a clerk at the Bureau of United States Patents, and became the first woman ever to work in Washington at a government office. She received a salary of $1,400 a year, the same salary the male clerks at the Patent Office were earning at the time. Many men felt threatened by her and foresaw a dangerous precedent in a woman being hired in place of a man. In the hallways she often had to endure rude stares and unkind remarks. One worker even spat tobacco juice on her as she walked by. But none of this discouraged her. She refused to leave and soon became a valued employee.

CLARA ENDURES RUDE STARES AT HER GOVERNMENT JOB

On April 14, 1861, the Civil War erupted and the United States became a divided nation. Union armies formed in the north to fight the Confederate armies of the South in a bloody exchange that was to last four years. Within hours after war was declared, federal troops began to pour into Washington. Clara heard that the 6th Massachusetts Infantry Regiment had arrived by train. The transport train had been attacked by Confederate sympathizers when it made a stop at Baltimore. Many of the soldiers were suffering from bruises and broken bones. During the attack, all the baggage was stolen. Troops were left with only the clothes they were wearing, which included long, woolen underwear that was unfit for the southern climate. Because of lack of space at the Washington infirmary, the wounded were taken to the Senate chamber at the Capitol. Knowing that some of her former students belonged to the regiment that was attacked, Clara decided to see if she could help.

The skills Clara learned as a child prepared her for her next move. She rushed home and packed baskets with food, eating utensils, and cotton underwear that she had bought with her own money. Then she hired five men to carry the supplies and marched with the men and supplies to the Capitol. A cheer went up when she entered the Senate chamber. At once, Clara knew her place in the war. She wrote to prominent officials in the War Department asking for permission to bring supplies to nurse the wounded at battle sites. Her request was granted.

AT THE CAPITOL, CLARA NURSES WOUNDED SOLDIERS FROM HER HOME STATE

Clara began her battlefield service in the summer of 1862 at Cedar Mountain in Virginia. She came to the rescue of Brigade Surgeon James I. Dunn, who had run out of supplies for the wounded. Clara arrived at the site with a wagonload of supplies. She got them by writing hundreds of letters asking the public for blankets, bandages, and medicine. Dunn called her "the Angel of the Battlefield," a name that caught on quickly.

Clara went on to other battlefields. Nothing stopped her from her mission. On foot, she crossed rope bridges that swayed and rocked as gunshot exploded around her. She tended the wounded and moved them to safety, before making a last-minute escape just as the Confederates came storming over the hill. She faced death many times. Her clothing became riddled with bullet holes. Once she stopped to give a fallen soldier a drink of water. As she cradled him in her arms, a bullet passed under her arm and hit the soldier, killing him instantly. She witnessed horrors of death and dying, starvation, and needless suffering at the Battle of Antietam, the Battle of Fredericksburg, and other major battle sites in Virginia.

In the spring of 1863, Clara moved on to Port Royal, near Charleston, South Carolina. There she continued to provide nursing care for soldiers on the battlefield. She was not paid for her services. She used her own money for her volunteer work, including savings from her earnings at the Patent Office and from an inheritance left by her father, who had died in 1862.

CLARA RUSHES SUPPLIES TO THE CIVIL WAR BATTLEFIELDS

When at last the Civil War ended in 1865, Clara still had work to do. She wrote a letter to President Lincoln, expressing her interest in establishing a bureau to trace missing soldiers. Lincoln granted her the authority—one of his final acts before his assassination on April 14, 1865. Over a period of four years, Clara helped to locate more than 22,000 missing soldiers. At the same time, she helped to establish a national cemetery at the site of the notorious Andersonville Prison in Georgia. Clara raised the national flag at the dedication ceremonies. The Confederacy had confined 33,000 Union soldiers at Andersonville Prison. Of these, 12,000 died from starvation, exposure, and disease. The prison was a symbol of murder, madness, and the senselessness of war. It reflected Clara's own nightmarish experiences on the battlefield. About Andersonville Prison she said, "Surely this was not the gate to hell, but hell itself."

Although Congress had given Clara some funds for her bureau, it was not enough to continue her work. In order to earn more money she was forced to make a lecture tour. From 1866 to 1868, she traveled all over northern and western United States giving hundreds of lectures. She became exhausted from traveling and reliving the horrors of the war through her presentations. After her doctor insisted that she quit and take a long rest abroad, Clara agreed to go to Geneva, Switzerland.

CLARA HOISTS THE FLAG AT THE NATIONAL CEMETERY AT ANDERSONVILLE

A GERMAN GUARD LETS CLARA GO ON TO SERVE THE WOUNDED IN FRANCE

While recuperating in Geneva, Clara heard of an organization called the International Red Cross that was dedicated to serving the wounded at battlefields. It was founded by a wealthy Swiss industrialist, Jean-Henri Dunant, who had served as a battlefield nurse in Italy. Red Cross volunteers, the wounded, their hospitals, conveyances, and supplies were considered neutral and safe from attack. The International Red Cross had been operating since the Geneva Convention of 1864, which set guidelines for the treatment of wounded soldiers and prisoners during war. Twelve foreign nations signed the Geneva Treaty.

In 1870, a war broke out suddenly between France and Prussia, a former German state that occupied most of north and central Germany. Because Clara's work during the Civil War was well known abroad, the Grand Duchess Louise of Baden, a patron of the Red Cross, asked her to organize relief for the conflict. At once, Clara forgot her illness and fled her sickbed. She crossed the border into France and went to Haguenau, where a battle was raging. A German guard was stopping people at the front lines. Quickly, Clara untied a red ribbon that she wore at her throat and sewed it to a strip of white cloth. She created a red cross on a white field—the International Red Cross emblem—and wore it as an armband. Seeing the Red Cross symbol, the guard let her pass. Clara went on to serve the wounded as a neutral agent in the Franco-Prussian War, which lasted ten months. Then, in 1873, she returned home.

After Clara returned to the United States, she could not forget her work with the Red Cross. She was eager to form a branch of the Red Cross in America that would aid victims of disaster in peacetime as well as war. In 1877, she wrote to Gustave Moynier, the current president of the International Red Cross, about her plan. He sent a letter for her to give to the twenty-seventh president of the United States, Rutherford B. Hayes. The letter established Clara as the U.S. Representative of the International Red Cross and asked that America sign the Geneva Treaty and organize a branch of the Red Cross. At once, Clara headed for Washington.

Hayes was not receptive to Clara's plan, nor was Congress. The long-standing belief of the time was that to sign treaties with Europe might lead to foreign countries meddling in U.S. affairs. However, when Chester A. Arthur was elected to the presidency four years later, Clara felt encouraged by the new administration and moved forward with her plan. Calling forth supporters and followers to her Washington apartment, she founded the American Red Cross Society on May 21, 1881. Clara was elected president of the society. Three months later, she organized the first Red Cross chapter in Dansville, New York, followed by one in Rochester and another in Syracuse, New York. A short time later, a tremendous fire broke out in northern Michigan and a flood occurred on the Ohio River. Clara's Red Cross came to the rescue.

CLARA'S RED CROSS SERVES VICTIMS OF A DISASTROUS FLOOD

Clara's rescue work during the disasters proved to President Arthur and Congress what the Red Cross could accomplish. As a result, the United States became the thirty-second member of the International Committee of the Red Cross. In response, Gustave Moynier sent out an official bulletin that said:

> "Without the energy and perseverance of this remarkable woman, Clara Barton, we should not for a long time have had the pleasure of seeing the Red Cross received in the United States."

Clara's strength lay in her ability to organize volunteers to aid disaster victims. In 1884, she organized steamers to take supplies to flooded families along the Mississippi and Ohio rivers. In 1888, she assisted stricken people in Jacksonville, Florida, during an outbreak of yellow fever. In 1889, she gave medical care to 25,000 victims of the Johnstown, Pennsylvania, flood. In 1893, she brought aid to victims of a hurricane at Sea Islands off the coast of South Carolina. Later that year, Clara, at age seventy-two, went to Turkey for ten months to help survivors of a religious war. In 1898, she went with a relief ship to Havana during Cuba's revolt against Spain. She lunched on the battleship *Maine* just two days before it was blown up, a disaster that led to the Spanish-American War. She stayed on in Cuba to aid victims of the War, including soldiers from Roosevelt's Rough Riders. Her Red Cross service over the years brought her international fame and medals and honors from world leaders.